Oncoming Traffic

Maakomele R. Manaka

First published by Botsotso in 2018

Box 30952
Braamfontein 2017

botsotso@artslink.co.za
www.botsotso.org.za

ISBN: 978-0-9947081-4-4

Acknowledgements

Versions of these poems have been previously published
in the following journals/magazines/websites: Aerodrome,
Best New African Poems, Botsotso, Illuminations, New Coin, Oir Ese Oir, Tyhini

Poems in Setswana edited by Sabata Mpho Mokae
Poem in isiZulu edited by Sabelo Soko
General editor: Allan Kolski Horwitz

"…the blues is you in me
I never knew the blues until I met you…"
Sipho Sepamla

Contents

ME

SILENCE

WE

ME

Self-Portrait

i am a horse
with a human face that
cannot look past its legs

i drink happiness
with a mourning cup

my babalaz mattress
knows the corpses
that write my poems

my soul is a township
of decomposing memories
that don't remember my feet

and still
                my palms itch

Bara

For Steve "Lavovo" Maubane

the Venda vendor
sits in a lotus position
conducting an orchestra
of languished fruits
and lonely cigarettes
gyrating ballerinas of cue marshals
command a mob of drivers clothed in clouds
of ganja smoke that sing:
      "Mina Ngi ya shunqa, mlungu"
the music of hair dryers
with diluted tales
jump out of Pelo's Hair Salon
and dance to the Ten Rand scent
of a slowly cooked skopo
outside Bara's barracks
decaying medicinal scent
and high hooters
marinate the air
school shoe rhythms
of uniform dreams
stomp the ground
while cockroaches of fat rats
invade the soil
covered in dog
and human vomit
closed liquor stores fill
with phuza faces
while I sharpen my voice
to knife my way through

Mphakathi

"Take her out of the house"/ "mme o, wa loya"/ "akana nhliziyo"/
"khiphani lo mgorho"/ "re gathetse ke yena, go neng"/ "Yaa!"/
"just burn the house down" / "e Sipho! kick her in the head" / "u
yenzeni lo mama?"/ "who do you think was responsible for Dijo's
death last week" / "tshisa daar ding maan"/ "wooo! modimo wa
maIsrael," / "bring her out here Thami" / "mercy batho bamodimo,
mercy"/ "hau morena" / "nxese, nxese" / "that's enough maAf-
rika, we cannot continue like this" / "tsamaya o lo joetsa magoa
matlakala ao, voetsek" / "khabani le nja" / "woo shem, na nka mo
dira Sipho" / "hahaha, how could you talk about that now maar le
wena Nthabiseng" / "just look at him, o fit maan" / "hlehla, hlehla
sisi" / "maponisa a fetlhile mama" / "I think it's a good thing my
boy" / "tjho tjho tjhooo!" / "eish, bo fadere are here now, le nna ne
ke batla go latlhela sengwe nyana, mmereko o ntene" / "no no no!
ntate leponisa, leave those boys alone, ha se bona" / "tyhini! kutheni
polis maan? ufika apha ngokugeza, thixo" / "dude, lets just go get
some weed ko renkeng, I've got that new Redman joint" / "bo gata
ba na ba beda" / "voetsek ngabo!" / "maAfrika, maAfrika thewu-
sang moya" / "do that at your house, let's get the weed, bra" / "no
no no, bantu benkosi nxese kodwa, asizwaneni labo baba benza u
msebe…"/ "tsamaya o lo djoetsa president masepa ao" / "Mama ke
tshwere ke tlala" / "ok nana, let's go, there is nothing those police
men can do now for that poor old lady, a re ye"

The Sky and the City

the tall sky walks
past short buildings
listening to court rooms
burning innocent feelings

steaming streams
of train tracks
run beneath a bridge
that cannot bridge
the voice of water

aging bottles
of slender figures
sell stale orgasms
to wet poles

the sky looks on
from a city that breathes
inside of a shoe
and knows
how the streets feel

the sky walks on
with a yawning eye
and stares at blue dragons
raiding silhouettes
of fingers trading heights
while ash-tray playgrounds
house brown songs
that are yet to grow

Take Away

take away
the pot of now
this rainbow
is empty

take away
the carpet between
history's thighs
when nameless cows
search for their sound

what will I feed
my unborn words
when this diseased cold
pages over old bones

tonight the spirit ink and I dance
the *Mokama** dance

so take away everything
everything that takes me away
away from staying
staying away from everything
that passes away

but please
don't take away
my sacrament
when Malombo is on
unplugging the rainbow

Mokama—a trance state inducing ritual dance by the San people

Poet of the Pavements:

The Autobiography of M R Manaka

i was born loud
on a reserved stage
in the heart of winter
on Mother's page

named grandfather before
i could father my name
and later i realized
the nameless cold
i had to father

at twelve an old man's wall
collapsed my universe
with remorseless bricks
crushing my back
only my mind survived

hospital is no joke
the smell of injured worlds
drenches even the food
the cries of grown men
haunt my childhood bed

it was the playwright
my father's fears
that punctured my nature

after we laid the last breath
of my legs to rest
time learned to crawl
and memory walked barefoot
on sharp and rugged nails

i was born again
as a dancer
on a volcanic stage
moving to the velvet rhythm
of my father's death

cut-off from my blood
isolated by tomorrow's promises
removed from society's trombone stare
the poet in me came of age
on raging pavements
that wrapped their arms
around pieces of
my caged feathers

at twenty-one
i birthed pages
filled with the weeps
of a twelve year old man

at twenty-two
the earthquakes
in my voice flew me
to foreign languages
*where people never say hallo**
and cities riddled
with the screams of history
*from way, way down below**

i made love to the Caribbean sunset
Angelina was my home in Cuba
• her beauty was my refuge
with eyes as blue as the Pacific

in Jamaica I was a star
and another Afrikan in Germany
learned to speak Spanish in a day
when Madrid almost drank me
passed out backstage

with a blonde Holland
between my thighs
discovered i can fly
with the ground as my sky

the sun continued to shine
on the coldest days of my life
Italy embraced the saxophone in my garden
and translated the second book
of my Blues

i fell in love with a snake woman
my friends ate into my sorrow
they lived off the sun
from the winter in my mug

i have been
        broke
                broken
and my soul
                broken into
I have lived amongst hungry wolves
made love to long-legged
mini-skirted women of the night
many of whom today
star the heavens

i am hustling life
for new memories
because I am not going back
to the hospital of my days
nor to the quiet marimba
of my father's hand
across Mother's face

i am not going back
to the 4 rooms of poverty
nor to the bitter gales
of my neighbour's jealousy

i have sinned
killed a smile
speared the laughter
of my first lover
skinned my dignity
in front of my brother

i am a boy learning
to *Man-Up** and keep up
if only father told me
easy does not come easy

***borrowed from Hugh Masekela's song titled If There's Anybody Out There*
**Man-Up—The title of a book by Carlos Andres Gomez*

Isandla se langa

unga shoni langa
amehlo ami akhathele

angisenawo amandla
wokuphuza indlala

sekungathi inhlupheko
ukudla kwase khaya

ngiqinise langa
impilo ayina zwelo

Song for the Time
For Heidi & Gareth

i know why
        you cannot sleep
you lay awake
watching your plans
wrestle the ceiling
with ears facing a k/night
        breathing on your feet

i have heard you
        ask for directions
from a yellow razor

i know you
        pray to exit
wounds that breed
self hatred

as for me
i pray for you to exist
in the soundless harmonies
of the many water-ways
inside your smiles

Letter to Art
For Sthu

Dear Art

i've been longing
to tell you this
especially now
when i look at the world
through your eyes

i miss you

i remember
how you would sit
and lounge reality
from the couch
with paint brushes
and red wine eyelashes
type-writing dawns
that would hold my ears

how can i forget
the look in your voice
when my brother told you
that i failed a semester
and how you responded
'Mokone never fails'
those words have kept
my nerve-endings together
for that thobela mokone

and after your
sudden departure
i remember
the sleepless bingeing
of my anger
i was confused
how could you leave
without even a whisper

about my other brother
but Art, my father
as a man still becoming
i understand why
you kept him a secret
it would've complicated
so many things

nonetheless, papa
the 12 year old man
still misses you

it has not been easy, papa
but i've begun to understand
how you saw life

ART is LOVE SUPREME

and looking at Sthu
i know it's possible

i am your eyes
and my brothers
your canvas
i can see
what they don't say
we long to hold giggling days
with you and her again

papa
please forgive my art
i write this from a mountainous road trip
en route to forgiving my self
now is not the same
i miss you more
                    now

Love always

            Your son

Silence in Literature

                    i am sorry Mama
i cannot tell you
                    what you want to hear

          i can see
                              my fear in your eyes
          your tongue like my feet
                              cannot stand the words
                                                  that steal
                                                        my ground

               i am trying Mama…

sometimes i lose myself
                    to question marks
                                   that ask:
"whose blood will carry this line?"

               i am sorry Mama
some words cannot outrun reality
          they do not allow us
to exhale
                    what we want to say

Bedsores

sometimes my legs lie to me
& bottle my smile
i have swallowed my eyes
& died behind the walls
of my laughter

i have silenced my shadow
when it was time to stand up

i have walked out on my body
and some day
my body will walk out
                            on me

Before I die

*(Inspired by Nicanor Parra's poem **The Poet Who Sleeps on the Chair**)*

blue page of many words
teaches me how to listen
to a poem written by the sea

i want to learn the ways of water
teach my ears how to swim
beyond monolingual rivers
that fail to recite the scent
of the ocean's black h/air

blue blanket of
my grandmother's song
teach my storm
how to voice your dance
so i can avalanche my way out
of ignorance

teach my stomach
to be resilient
against the sloth
that consumes my tongue
urging my pen
to follow mediocrity

mother of many blank pages
teach me how to write the rain
on open palms of your sea

The Stove

she was old
rusted
and grey
yet her warmth
brought us closer

her hot voice
filled the kitchen
even the pots
loved her touch

i was raised
by her laughter
taught how to walk
in the yellow shoes
of her radiant beam

after the kitchen floor grew
she was the first to move
old and charcoaled with humility

now we no longer laugh
she has become a painting
brightening the barriers
                of our memory

Open Road

the road opens homes
it holds painful potholes
of endless debts
highways to
countless dead-ends

it shoulders days
that breast-feed scars
with phuza faces

it opens wounds
of withering widows
that remember the
killing of smiles
behind proud windows

eGazini

two leave and only one returns
far from the 11 blue notes
of *Hungry Flames**
and the busy buzz of Bara
the fragrance of my Zone-6 departs
carrying a bass-line childhood

the air is different   here
the land feels off
and time has a beat of its own
here where history
is trapped in the stones
and not in the Mfengo soil
the settlers settled even in the blood

feels as though home is very far   here
yet across the weary hills
i hear my grandmother whispering
"Tsamaya o lo batla bophelo ngwanaka"

*Hungry Flames — title of an anthology of short stories

25

Moving into Another Life

lap-top crash
cellphone screen smash
everything out of tune
nothing connects
panic eats me
           but
my Mother is god

anxiety chains our tears
all we do is wave
sad eyes of unsaid goodbyes
my brother sits next to me
& shoulders my fears
warbling melodic wheels
ground his head into the headrest
the pitch black night
consumes us all
                  except me

the morning-breeze
sneaks across my feet
second drop-off is us
a whiskey friend of a friend
waits, greets and meets
my brother and i

we drive and search
                but
only bad timing
accommodates us
panic eats me again
breakfast at Spur
only my Black Label
can fill the hungry
desperation
of uncertainty
              but

panic eats
even the black
brain-freeze!
quick airtime fix
phone call overdose
                    my Mother is god

finally
a home finds me

my brother and i
stand on our tears

Broke Pockets

inside my pockets
thin cows bruise a mountain's knees
& sketch blue spaceships
for a penny-less universe

my patient lips pepper
the waiting of chili papers
but engine failures outside my pockets
unfold black winters

Pirate Suns

on naked gardens
memory is a plantation
reciting intimate suns
& sweating salty secrets
of unspoken moons

O garden of memory
please teach my plants
how to recall her sunrise

Remember Fezisa

For Fezisa Mdibi

somewhere
in the oceanic forest
between hills & dreams of
weeping streams

between waking up
& not knowing
the difference

my mermaid love
fails to breathe

The N12 Blues

For Senzo

inside the smoking noise
the three-piece band
breaks through the city's marrow
with a quiet funk
and a bass-line smirk

the silent snare recollects
how the troubled trombone
would piano water
to the conga hunger
with an upright patience

starving midnight notes
on the N12 highway
wait for the thirsty trio
to finish jazzing food
for full tables
while their stomachs
peruse the percussive
                    emptiness

inside today's noise
my beat bleeds
for the passing
of a friendly baseline

If I Could Sing
For ntate Hugh

write me a song
about the elusive music
of a woman's thong

write me a song
about the hard music
of a single parent's spinal fluid

write me a song
about the blind poet
who recites music

write me a song
about the bump and grind
of a musician's plight

write me a song
about a ghetto ballerina
who sees the song and hears the dance

write about the notes of dead flutes
and the unfair dirt
on our soldiers' boots

write me a song
about the haunting cries
of a Griqua's declining smile

write me a symphony
about the unheard misery
inside the soil's history

write me a song
about a father's worn out shoes
a mother's unfruitful womb

but before you write me out
of this chord progression
teach me how to write *your* song

Bloodlines in the River
For Kaone & Tile

the river of my road
leaves my Mother
feeling clueless and stuck

my brother struggles to listen
but I see tomorrow's unending embers
in the rivers within his eyes

i listen to my father's road
sounding me to sober
the river inside my walls

"Remember the river
in your blood, my son"
                  he bellows
from graveyards
in the sky
looking at how
        stuck
my river has become

Bophelo Ke Ntwa
For Sthu and Ben

i am that bird
                    that flies
          backwards
hoping
          to touch
                    sunrise

"there is no shame in failure!"
          shouts
                              my grandmother
                    from feathers
          misplaced
in today's flight

                              bophelo ke ntwa
                    a war zone
          in the mirror
                                        self
                    is the enemy

                              i am that bird
                    that flies backwards
          through barriers
of grandfathers' clouds
                              hoping to find my place
                    on the page

Grazing Past

only
                    the water-tanks remember
the famished corners
of township Decembers

only
                    the water-tanks remember
kitchens cooking laughter
lazy lines at the spaza

only
                    the water-tanks remember
black-mampatile every hour
the shoeshine-piyano of 1 pala
the sunshine of midnight lovers

only
          my
                    feet
                              remember
the water-tanks
in father's eyes

the amputation of balance

Mokone

*(After Chris Van Wyk's poem **Me and the Rain**)*
For Me

i want to
unfold my heart
into a calabash
& pour life onto my toes
rain with the sky
& dance on wet roads
with *pula* in my bones

i want to
pull down idle walls
inside my spinal cord
& rebuild recording rooms
for muscles that forgot how to talk
teach my crutches
how to unclasp my legs
when *pula* liberates
the mbira in my walk

i want to
dig a grave
for slender nights
that carry earthquakes
of Mother's cancer cries
unlearn the wine of pride
& marimba *pula*
to my brother's heaven

i want to
speak with horns
on my tongue
pushing rivers out my palms
with the rhythms of Bakone
standing on *Tlhantlhagane's* shoulders
shouting

pula!

pula!

pula!

Shi

For her

Badimo ba nkutlwile
Ngwatle wa Malebogo
molema phatshimo
ka loleme

MmaSeema
ke kopa o ntheetse
nnete ke seretse
botshelo ke semphekgo
o se fele pelo
fa botshelo
bo gata ditoro
ke tsoga
ke se na maatla
a mafoko

Moshibudi
morata lerato
ntshepe
ke tshipi ya thaba
molatela segametsi
legotlo la Barolong
moja Tlhapi
le Mpofana
ke Tlhantlhagane
ya ga mme le rre

tshidisano
ga e bonolo
lelapa le a berekelwa
kutlwano ke lenyalo
la dinonyane
le legodimo
'kgomo tsa me
ke ditiro

'rato la mafoko a Lowe
a re iteboge ka tlotlo
fa re nwa ditshego
tsa bosigo

mma go Botshelo
motshwara tladi molala

badimo ba nkutlwile
mafifi a maloba
ga a sa ntwantsha

Moshibudi
Ngwatle ya Themba
o magetla
a lefatshe la me

SILENCE

Oncoming Traffic

as the hardworking sun
lays its eye to rest
homes turn into liquor stores
behind church walls
pakistani shops feed
last minute groceries

mothers pray
in search of a god
desperation holds
candlewax tears
in a spineless room
with children buried
beneath brown beds
of homemade porn

i listen to the on-
coming traffic dust
of desperation
giant exhibitions
of funeral parlors
after-tears of fading years
my neighbor's rotting grin
the deafening flames
of teenage pregnancy

the traffic
keeps coming
over a woman's
silent yell for help
street bashes of AIDS
yet nobody wants to dance
on a gunman's open skull
in front of his mother's house

my uncle's explosive drinking
trying to hide the traffic
my grandmother's quiet anger
the relative who always
expects a hand out
the hungry spoiled child
who is never full

home is
the oncoming pus
oozing out
of Christmas dinners
the helpless gaze
of carrying on

WE

Children Born of Children

*(After Ingoapele Madingoane's **Africa My
Beginning** and **Khumbula, My Child**)*

from the new sound of an old breath
we learnt how to sing
inside the spear
of a foreign tongue

we taught ourselves how to love
within the walls of our ocean
and raised midnights
to reasonable mornings
hoping the river
will remember our poems

we wrote our names with water
when our hands could no longer
carry the resistance in our stones

    Khumbula my child!

our hands shouted inside the spear
of a foreign page
surrounded by silver faces
and the loud smoke
of coal trains

    Khumbula my child!

our songs silenced time
from the palm
of a mine dump

    Khumbula my child!

Black Day
For Dambudzo

look how normal their white tongues
have become inside your mouth
while a wave of black bodies
labor across compounds
of barren fields hoping
the Black Sunlight*
will expose
their wounds

Black Sunlight—title of Dambudzo Marechera's novel

The Nihilismus of a Black *Dahdah* (Duck)
(After Amiri Baraka's Black Dada Nihilismus)

he tries to talk
but his words do not know him
his words do not exist
but he exists in those words
this *dahdah* makes no sense

he tries to move
but his mind cannot walk
his feet are not fast enough
to outrun the madness in his words
he loathes the skin
he is wearing
his words lost their voice
in the kwaito of hunger
the hunger for acceptance
but never for self

he runs and rants
with holes in his speech
and plastic hands too weak
to carry the cries of his heritage

nihil is his mind
he doesn't trust his mother's songs
songs that air memory
to his lungs
Dada!
stop confusing blackness with poverty
                    Black
          'you are on your own'
but never alone
before sound birthed rhythm
we ate mala mogodu
from nature's calabash

black is not the color of your skin
black is the sky after the sun sleeps
the music that swallows darkness
your mother's breath of love

O Captain! My Captive

(Title inspired by W. Whitman's **O Captain! My Captain**)
For BK, KK, & Bisto

O captain
my captain
our fears have come
the last call is here

our unpaid languages
flood the bar
with homeless beers
lubricating volcanoes
in our brains

there are not enough
blue glasses
to hold whiskey clouds
when the emptiness
reigns from the ground

there are no more poems
for you to drink
my pockets
have run out of ink

o captain!
my captive
the fearless journey
has begun
i am tired of
drinking my cows
when will you let go
of my tomorrow?

Waiting for Sanity
For papa Ramps and Mothofela

the canvas is patient
it anticipates the waiting
it knows how to wait
the violent waiting
of a promise
& the two-faced silence
that comes with patience

the canvas remembers
it waits for walls
to remember
the waiting of a lie
and the masks
behind the waiting

the canvas bleeds
the patience of always
                          waiting
waiting to swallow
the sleepless hunger
in the eyes of
its infant colors

     waiting

               waiting
       to be called
                     waiting
for money
that has no legs
                     waiting
for days
that cannot stand
                     waiting
for a shot
that cannot warm the soul

9 to 5
For Shi

the sun mumbles its way
past a thick layer
of taxi-rank laughter
and cuts into the melanin
of migrant bees
shuffling through
the bitter-sweet blues
of yesterday's news

wingless birds sing of cages
running on borrowed muscle
the sultry struggle
of the mid-month hustle
warbling wheels wane time
traffic is life
at this corner of sunrise

9 to 5
five to cloud-nine
through the debts
past the heat of long lines
from Monday to December
endless debit orders crutch
on my lover's legs
and tombstones her face

at the blackest sound
just before the sun stumbles
past humble curtains
i watch my lover once more
swallow the music of death

House Music

For Nathidread

do homeless people listen
to house music?
or do they dance to
whatever jive's leftover

oh cow-n-tree of robots
look at the drought
in your song

we are chained cheetahs
still dreaming of running
beautiful humming birds
without a sense of harmony

unlanguaged children
dancing to music
refusing to house notes
forging new tones

modimo ke paki
coz in the mouths
of cunning fools
mediocrity is food

Born to the Blackness

For Lefifi Tladi, Lesego Rampolokeng and Masello Motana

> *Hey there mpintshi*
> *Homeless in your home*
> *Gaona batswadi*
> *Let me help you stand*
> *I know that it's hard*
> *I know it's been hard*
> *But tomorrow is in your hand*

oh Black god
of Black truth

how long must the
colorless arrogance
continue to bleach
the Black speech
with beer halls of amnesia
always expecting us
to jive to the jive
this unforgiving jive
this pale pasty
and impaling jive of
> *"move on!"*
> *"let's get along!"*
when the marrow
of Black days
still chokes
on white bones

when so many
idioms inside
the sad soil
remain rearranged
and relocated

when Black waters
keep disappearing

and descending
deeper
into this open grave
passing burials of
Black songs
digging and drilling
the nothingness
in search of bophelo

how many times
should Black roses
assume 'the position'
while gutless ears
pretend the flaring silence
does not exist?

but something happened
yes, something is happening

> *Hey there mpintshi*
> *Homeless in your home*
> *Gaona batswadi*
> *Let me help you stand*
> *I know that it's hard*
> *I know it's been hard*
> *But tomorrow's in your hand*

oh black man
of black pain

for how long
must you be
homeless at home
how much of you
do you even own?

why must Blackness
begin with defeat

Hey there ntwana
Gcwal'ibruko lakho
Remember who you are
You are not a fool
I know it's been hard
I know that it's hard
But
Lomhlaba nawe ngowakho

Leano on My Mind

the winter star
of this black morning
burns in flames of a childhood
the ghetto cannot forget

breathless streets
suffocating families
living inside a mine-dump
and drilling their way to sleep

the ghetto knows how to remember
the smiles of little men
whose windows hold dying candles
searching for a hole in the ground

yet when i look at my niece Leano
i know that from an avalanche of rocks
a flower can still blossom

The Ill/Literate Flag
For Atli, Omolemo & Leano

in my country
education is dangerous
higher learning guns
shoot young tongues
with curriculums
they cannot afford

uniformed blue orders
shamelessly teargas dreams
& barricade innocent pages
with barbwires of rage

i wonder if people
who wield power
have children too
do they also bite
the same dues?

families on the periphery
barely breaking bread
forced to pay fees
for rooms of clustered class rooms
underpaid stuff overworked
with not enough textbooks

for how long
will power crucify
the truth about
whose culture is really
tilling the soil?

i feel like
the only black
on our flag
                isolated
and stifled
by other colors
coz in my country
even my skin
is illiterate

Memory is Blood
For ntate Don & ntate Kgositsile

for us whose names
were auctioned at birth
shot out of wedlock
and sold to the literature
of belt marks and kaffir-klaps

Memory is blood

coz every house
holds exhibitions
of blood stained memorials

in the presence
of today's abbreviated
cult-u-re in-boxing the present
we are mine-dumps
migrating in the dust

memory for sale!
memory for sale!
log in or sign up…
to the social status
that drinks it's own blood

Amnesia is the weapon

uphi umkhonto?
coz even after a
century of land theft
isakhala le nkomo

whose liter/atchar
will my child inherit?
when our education is anaemic

to be so German-cut off
we have no access
to the poetry
of our own hair

for us who remember
the auctioning of memory
our life-liquids dwell in the sewers
fighting amnesia

During the Drought

i was the voiceless
listening to foreign footprints
teething tears
inside a native yard

i was the wind
shouting 'Izwe Lethu'
to sleeping corpses
dreaming of dying
and waking up to death

i was the cracking sound
of a heart breaking
away from it's self
only to try piece itself together

when the drought found me
i was a boy hiding in the wardrobe
praying that men with lifeless weapons
will not come in the house
cut open our love
and parade our innards
around the tip of their pangas
like pieces of jewelry

i was my grandmother's feet
standing in the drought's heat
searching for alms
inside the ballot
of a broken street

when the Rain began
i was the load-shedding winter
on a blackout table
surrounded by candle lights
trying to escape a closed window

when the Rain came
i became the normalized
rage caged within
screaming for acceptance

in the name of 'Rainbow'

Of My Republic

*(After Dambudzo Marechera's poem **Raid**)*

at the floor
of this Black beer
freedom stirs
endless loans
repossessing stars
worlds of joy
collapse a full glass
happiness drowns
skeleton lips

at the bottom
of black beds
i have witnessed
gay flowers blossom
into lesbian suns
beneath bellowing blankets
inside a room full
of conservative shoes
trying to preserve
policies of
cultural perverts

on the split floor of
this black spit
slavery sells daylight
with cold quarts
mining the heat
inflation sits on rocks
& strips the sand
down to its socks

at the core of
our banana republic
blackness drinks endlessly
*for revolutionary spells**

trying to keep from sinking
into the born-free credit
poison pulse party politics

at the bottom of
my black salvation
any liquor
will do

*a line borrowed from James Mathews poem

Ke Kopa Metsi!

For malome Philip Tabane

'sedi la me
nkapese pula
ke nyorilwe letlalo

mmu ke madi
madi ke botlhoko

lefatshe ke metsi
metsi ke botshelo
botshelo ke loso
gae

Modimo ke nyorilwe
ke kopa metsi

Maropeng

For mama

thipa ga e na botlhale / pelong ya tlou / lerato la mme le bogale /
go itse barapedi ba ntwa / ba ba neng ba khunama / fa a na kgalema
sefako sa boloi / ka sebete maotong / a gata dipoko tsa botlhoko ka
tladi / peo se lebale matsogo a mme / maru a gompieno ga a ithate.

Angazi but I am Sure

For malome Reuel Khoza

five-finger

Art can

lies off the constitution's face

vice-grip

the privileged snow
and remove

di kitshini

from our mothers' shoes

blue-eye

the

"Baas-turd"

statues on our tongues

June-July

them
until they move out

throw

"guava-juice"

poems at the

check-no-coast

government

angazi but I'm sure

art can

stop-nonsense

the young yard
from consuming
self

A.B.C Rap

after all the applause our art remains alien / barricaded by barren
bootleggers of belligerent ballots / constantly collecting coins and
content from a constellation of creative citizens who are not content
/ while dare devils deliberately drown dreams of their descendants
/ exhuming extinct emotions only for entertainment's eccentric ex-
pectations / followers of forgotten folk tales flower your selves from
fallacy / gamble not with gods' gratitude & gravitate your goals to
greatness / heal homes with honesty / intertwine intellectual inner
sense with integrity / jab jet legged jaws of power junkies with jus-
tice / kill them with a kaleidoscope of kindness / let art lead through
layers of lies that loop life to loneliness / masquerading as meaning-
ful members of society while migrating masses to the land of milk
and madness / note the nonsense in nodding when nations neglect
nationalism / occupying octaves and overstepping originality / poi-
son pulp pulse in veins writes the poet / quarantined street quartets
question the parliament's queer art with quills / readily reeling on
rails of the economy's rusty rims / seems sad to say this but sincerity
amongst artists is sliding sideways / though through transparency
can we triumph & transcend this timid tapestry / urging us to ululate
a urinated unity / venting votes for voices of venomous villains and
vixens / X marks the unknown xylophones born in exile / while
we wallet wails of waiting / yesterday's youth yearns for sounds of
yesteryear meanwhile today's future yawns / & only zealots of the
unlanguaged art can zoom the zeitgeist zoo out of these zenith zones
of phobia.

Earth, Wind and Hunger

there are winds
the moon does not want to share
winds of molested rivers
and a tired ocean

there are songs
the moon cannot dance to
crying black flames
on starving mountains

there are winds
the moon does not want to remember

Poetry's Last Breath

For Funda Centre

don't bury me
burn me

let the wind
voice my ashes
to sterile ears

let your wounds
ink my body
when you burn me
into your memory

don't bury me
learn my sound
hear the ashes
sing riverbed tales
to your children's names

Maakomele R. Manaka is a Soweto born poet with a strong artistic heritage. South African icon, Dr. Don Mattera says, "If genius can be genetically connected and if it flows from generation to generation, then Mak Manaka is the epitome of it. He comes from a dynasty of talented, creative and gifted people Nomsa and Matsemela". Mak, as he is widely known, has published three collections of poetry *If Only* (self published, 2003. Edited by Don Mattera) and *In Time* (Geko,2009. Edited by Andrew Miller) and *Flowers Of A Broken Smile* (Inksword, 2016); two of which have been translated into Italian and German. His writings have appeared in literary journals and news papers globally and around the country: Mail & Guardian, Aerodrome, New Coin, Botsotso, Kotaz, The Chronic, Poetry Potion, Best New African Poets and Illuminations. He also recorded a dub-poetry album titled, *Word Sound Power*. Manaka has been invited to perform his poetry at various literary festivals locally and abroad, from Soweto to Spain, Cuba, Jamaica, Lesotho, Botswana, Germany, Holland, Italy, Switzerland and at the inauguration of former president Mr. Thabo Mbeki; he also performed for the late Mr. Nelson Mandela. He received "best art of the year" at the age of 5 at the once celebrated Funda Art Centre, and was nominated for The Daimler Chrysler Poet Of the Year 2005 Award. He represented South Africa at the closing ceremony of the 2006 FIFA World Cup in Germany and performed at the Market Theatre in 2018 for a tribute show to South African icons titled *The Living Legends*. Manaka teaches creative writing in and around South Africa and holds a Masters Degree in Creative Writing from Rhodes University.

Printed in the United States
By Bookmasters